WESTON-SUPER-MARE
IN OLD PHOTOGRAPHS
1950s

WESTON-super-MARE
IN OLD PHOTOGRAPHS
1950s

COLLECTED BY
SHARON POOLE

Budding
BOOKS

A Budding Book

First published in 1991 by Alan Sutton Publishing Limited

This edition published in 2001 by Budding Books,
an imprint of Sutton Publishing Limited
Phoenix Mill · Thrupp · Stroud · Gloucestershire GL5 2BU

A catalogue record for this book is available from the British Library

ISBN 1-84015-195-1

Typesetting and origination by
Sutton Publishing Limited.
Printed in Great Britain by
J.H. Haynes & Co., Sparkford.

CONTENTS

THE COVER of the 1951 guide to Weston-super-Mare. This was a special design by Grafton Arts of London for the year of the Festival of Britain. Forty thousand copies were printed – less than usual as there was still a paper shortage after the Second World War.

INTRODUCTION

Why devote a whole book to Weston-super-Mare in the 1950s? The initial impetus came while looking through a collection of photographs in Woodspring Museum, mostly taken during the year 1958. Thirty-three years is by no means a long time and well within many people's memories yet, seeing those pictures, I was struck by how different life is now. This applies as much to visible evidence, such as architecture, cars and clothing as to society itself. The 1950s were a period of great change, both nationally and locally. After the end of the Second World War there was a restlessness. People had new ideas and values, and it became a period of rebirth and renewal. Many changes took place during this decade as the country emerged from a time of austerity to mass consumerism. It was this difference in life between 1950 and 1960 that led me to compile this visual record. My first book, *Weston-super-Mare in Old Photographs*, covered over a century, and it was a great challenge to confine the selection this time to a single decade. However, I hope this book will be just as interesting and varied.

The 1950 General Election saw the post-war Labour Government returned, but with a greatly reduced majority. In the autumn of 1951 the Conservatives took office under Winston Churchill, and set about a programme to lift any remaining wartime restrictions and controls, and to increase exports. They also concentrated on relieving the housing shortage: Local authorities were given a national target of building 300,000 homes a year.

The Second World War was still very much in evidence long after peace was declared. Soap was rationed until 1950, identity cards were not abolished until 1952, and food rationing continued until 1953. Most towns also had their share of bomb sites as a daily reminder.

To encourage the nation towards rebuilding a future, the Festival of Britain was held in 1951. This was intended to celebrate Britain's achievements and stimulate British industry. Youth culture was born: the word 'teenager' was first used in the 1950s; young people had money to spend for the first time due to full employment and increased wages; rock and roll, coffee bars and young fashion emerged; and the single and LP record were developed, often played on the now classic 'Dansette' record-player. This emphasis on youth was underlined when King George VI died on 6 February 1952, and Princess Elizabeth became queen at the age of twenty-five.

The 1950s saw growth in many of the modern industries because the war had boosted development, particularly in the field of electronics. In 1954 television spread to a second channel, although it was still very much a novelty to most people. Transistors and computers became commercially feasible for the first time. The first nuclear power station opened at Calder Hall in 1956, and the decade saw the decline in the use of steam on the railways in favour of diesel and electricity. Farming became more mechanized and intensive, and many people left the land to work in new industries.

Weston-super-Mare in the 1950s, in common with many other towns in the country, had to rethink its direction and plan for the future. No longer could British seaside resorts rely on families booking their annual week by the sea when increasing disposable income and developments in air transport were making resorts abroad accessible. Bomb sites still punctuated Weston's streets and this, combined with a general feeling of wanting to wipe away the past and look to the future, led towards large-scale redevelopment plans being drafted. These were the first real changes to the face of Weston since it was first built in the nineteenth century.

In 1947 a report was drawn up by Clough Williams-Ellis and Lionel Brett, on Post-War Redevelopment. It advocated sweeping changes involving demolition and then rebuilding to a town plan, 'What remains of old Weston is so fragmentary that it must be written off where it conflicts with the general reconstruction scheme . . .' The town was at a crossroads. Already the newspapers reported heated debates over the reconstruction or redevelopment of bombed areas. This was brought to a head over the 'Battle of Waterloo Street'. This area had probably suffered more than any other in Weston and Lance & Lance's store on the south-east corner of High Street had been destroyed. It was suggested an 80 ft dual carriageway replace Waterloo Street, by swinging north along Worthy Place and meeting the sea front at West Street. Other town centre bomb sites included the Boulevard Congregational Church, parts of Orchard Street, Marks & Spencer's High Street store and parts of Union and Oxford Streets. By contrast, however, some areas of the town were still virtually unaltered from the early twentieth century. Small independent specialist shops still formed the bulk of the retail areas. Self-service supermarkets first opened in the 1950s and the large multiples had not yet turned the High Street into a copy of every other high street in the country.

Weston Borough Council wanted to make improvements by redeveloping a large area in the centre of the town. This, however, caused some controversy as it involved the demolition of some 119 domestic properties. The council put compulsory purchase orders on Carlton Street, Little Carlton Street, Castle Street, New Street, Sidmouth Cottages East and West, Maine Square, Atlantic Cottages and Shaddick's Cottages.

The dispute dragged on for years. In August 1957 a group was set up by the residents of the affected area. Known as the League of Home Defence, their aim was to fight against the clearance orders and to bring as much publicity to the issue as possible. The editorial in the *Weston Mercury* in November 1957 wrote, 'Weston's motto may be "Ever Forward" but that does not give us the undisputed right to push ahead in a reckless "damn the consequence's attitude".'

The two main causes of upset were the dispersal of the community and the fact that the houses had been declared 'unfit for human habitation'. Most of the residents were aged between fifty-two and eighty-nine and, in some cases, had lived there all their lives. They were therefore upset at having their homes called slums. They were also unhappy at being offered council houses at Earlham Grove, Milton and Oldmixon, as they were all some distance from the town centre. A public enquiry was held in 1957 as fifty-six objectors registered their opposition to the plan. A year later the decision by the Minister of Housing gave temporary reprieve to fifty properties. Demolition began on the remainder.

In 1961 Chamberlain, Powell & Bon were appointed to prepare designs for a wide-scale redevelopment of these areas, based on the town's continuing expansion of population, light industry and future tourism needs. The plan covered an area of over 7 acres, to be developed with a 200-bed hotel, conference centre, new library, 400-seat cinema, flats, shopping arcade, town hall extension and car parking.

In the event financial backing could not be obtained for the scheme and none of the Chamberlain, Powell & Bon design was implemented. The site was subsequently developed to form the Dolphin Square shopping precinct and Carlton Street car park.

This, however, was not the only part of the town scheduled for clearance and development. Union Street had already been widened, and new Government offices built on the east side. Plans for this area included shops and a multi-storey car park and involved the demolition of Laura Buildings, Wilcox Place, Regent Place and part of Regent Street.

Housing and car parking were deemed the major priorities as the population was growing rapidly. In 1931 it stood at 28,554; by 1951 it was 40,165. The war had brought much industry to Weston, including aircraft manufacture. Afterwards many of these industries stayed in the town and switched over to making peacetime products. Others left vacant factory premises. A case in point was the Bristol Aircraft Factory. This had been established as a production centre for the Bristol Beaufighter. When the war ended the factory transferred to manufacturing prefabricated aluminium bungalows to combat the initial housing shortage. When that was solved they started to make larger buildings such as schools, hospitals, etc. These were exported as far away as Australia. They also went on to make civil aircraft parts for the Bristol Britannia for BOAC. In 1958 the Borough Council decided to actively promote Weston as a base for light industry in order to provide a broader range of employment opportunities. The Town Development Act of 1952 had been passed to facilitate the movement of people and industry from overpopulated parts of the country. Under the Act, Weston used its long association with the Midlands to encourage some firms to move to Weston. The Council offered to sell or lease sites or buildings along Winterstoke Road at Oldmixon. Council housing was also made available for those workers wishing to move here.

The car-parking problem was harder to solve. The motor car became the symbol of the 'never had it so good' syndrome — the luxury that became a necessity. Petrol rationing was lifted in 1950 and the number of vehicles on the road rose from just over three million in 1939 to ten million in 1959. At the beginning of this period there was no permanent off-road car parking in Weston. All that was available were cleared war-damaged sites providing approximately 390 spaces. Conservative estimates of future needs were one thousand spaces, much of these to come from car parks in Palmer Street (also due for clearance), Carlton Street and Union Street.

If the above descriptions give the picture of Weston-super-Mare as a town of ill-feelings buried under piles of rubble and scaffolding this is not entirely accurate. Despite the rebuilding going on, residents and tourists were well catered for during the decade. In 1951 the town boasted three cinemas, the Central, Regent and Odeon, and four theatres, The Playhouse, Knightstone Theatre and, in the summer only, Madeira Cove Pavilion and The Arena, a marquee with a horseshoe-shaped stage, situated in Ellenborough Park South. In addition to the open-air pool and Knightstone swimming baths, Knightstone Medicinal Baths offered foam, vapour, hot seawater and seaweed baths. At Weston Airport, Western Airways ran a daily service to Cardiff, summer pleasure flights and air taxis to any part of Britain. Steamers sailed from Birnbeck Pier throughout the summer. The events of the day were covered by two weekly newspapers — the *Weston Gazette* and *Weston Mercury*.

All this gives a picture of a busy and thriving resort. It certainly provides food for thought when in 1990 Weston has only one theatre, one cinema (albeit with three screens), one newspaper and no air or sea services.

Enough now of facts and figures and on to the photographs. I hope they provide you with as much pleasure as I have had collecting them and making the following selection.

Sharon Poole 1991

Sun, Sea and Sand

WESTON SANDS, August 1959. Children make friends with this new arrival on the beach.

THE SEA FRONT and hillside at Weston, 1952. This photograph was taken from the roof of the Winter Gardens Pavilion.

THE TOURIST INFORMATION BUREAU, 1958. This mock-Tudor building was replaced in 1973 by the present information centre.

WHIT MONDAY, 26 May 1958. In these photographs teenagers are seen arriving in Weston at the Locking Road Excursion Station.

THE SANDS AND GRAND PIER, 1959. The pony carrige is called 'Weston Bomber', a reminder of the war.

THE SANDS TRAIN, 1954. This motorized, streamlined train first began operating at Whitsun of this year.

ARE YOU THE NEXT MARILYN MONROE? This beauty contest was held on the sands by the *Sunday Pictorial* in July 1957.

THE SANDS FIRE ENGINE, photographed in August 1952.

PUNCH AND JUDY SHOW, 1952. A crowd has gathered for this ever popular seaside attraction.

THE PUTTING GREEN at the Winter Gardens, 1952. Part of the Royal Arcade can be seen over the high wall.

CHOOSING THAT ALL IMPORTANT POSTCARD TO SEND HOME, 10 July 1958.

KNIGHTSTONE ROAD. Holiday-makers rest opposite the Melrose Café (now the Old Colonial Hotel).

THE PROMENADE. Two girls stop near the Grand Pier, for a shoeshine.

ENTRANCE TO THE GRAND PIER, 1953. This photograph was taken from the Grand Central Hotel. Knightstone can be seen in the distance.

ENTRANCE TO THE GRAND PIER at night, 1959.

THE BEACH LAWNS' FOUNTAIN, 1950. The old Edwardian cast ironwork has here been modernized with floodlights and plastic banding round the basins.

THE BEACH LAWNS' FOUNTAIN, from the Grand Central Hotel, July 1953. The two buses are advertising Simons' and Georges' beers. The little booth in front of the toilets is where 'Jackson's Faces' postcards were ordered. These superimposed a photograph of your own face in a corner of a viewcard of Weston.

BANK HOLIDAY CROWDS, 5 August 1957. Unlike today, when cars provide the main form of transport, most of these people would have arrived by train at the Excursion Station in Locking Road.

FOOTBALL GAME in the Grand Pier Pavilion, Sunday 14 July 1957.

PLAYING BINGO on the Grand Pier, 18 June 1957.

THE MARINE LAKE, 1950. The Marine Lake was built in 1927, in order that the tide would always be in on one part of the beach. Weston has the second largest tidal range in the world, and a day excursionist might never see the sea. The scheme also included widening the promenade and creating the walkway underneath. The pool was used for boating and bathing and was the largest of its kind in the country.

THE MARINE LAKE, 1952. This young lad is preparing to take out one of the manually-operated paddle-boats.

NOAH'S ARK. Marine Lake, 1954. This boat took visitors on a circuit of the lake.

A CORNER of the Marine Lake, August 1955. The van belonged to the Ray Ellington Quartet, who were performing at Knightstone Theatre.

A GAME OF GIANT DRAUGHTS, Easter Monday 1956. This board was on the sands by Marine Lake and can also be seen in the centre of the picture above.

'KIDDIES EXPRESS', 1952. This was one of the children's amusements at the Marine Lake.

'SPOT FLOOK AND WIN A GUINEA', so reads the banner on the railings. This *Daily Mail* cartoon character is seen here distributing prizes for a sandcastle competition at the Marine Lake, July 1956.

THE MARINE LAKE, 1952. Two views of amusements in the children's playground.

DONKEYS were as popular as ever in the 1950s. Here, Happy and Pepe take two little boys for a ride.

THE SANDS, 1958. Children are playing on the pleasure-boat landing-stages by the Grand Pier.

'ANYONE FOR THE *SKYLARK?*' Passengers board a pleasure-boat at Knightstone slipway for a trip round the bay. The boats used were flatners, a type of local craft used for fishing in winter. The name comes from their flat bottoms and shallow draught, which enabled them to reach the nets on an ebbing tide.

A TRIP ROUND THE BAY, 1958. This pleasure-boat is leaving from one of the beach landing-stages.

THE MARINE LAKE, 1954. The large gabled house is Glentworth Hall. It was built in the early nineteenth century by Richard Parsley, an early developer of Weston. It has since been replaced by a block of flats. The lamp-posts along the roadside once carried tram cables. The smoke in the distance is from the gas works.

WESTON LIGHT ORCHESTRA, 1952. Conducted by Lemuel Kinsey, they are playing in the Rozel Bandstand.

A QUEUE to get into the Rozel Bandstand, 1955. Admission was 6d. (2½p) for the 3p.m. performance and 1s. (5p) for the evening entertainment.

A PACKED AUDIENCE at the Rozel Bandstand, 1955.

BIRNBECK PIER. A paddle-steamer can be seen leaving the jetty.

KNIGHTSTONE BATHS, 1958. This indoor swimming-pool was built in 1902. There is a statue of a knight over the entrance. When the first medicinal baths were built in 1820 a skeleton was discovered and legend held that this was the Roman knight who gave the island its name. Early manuscripts, however, spell the island's name 'Nitestone', probably after the black appearance of the wet rock, a more likely origin of the name.

ANCHOR HEAD, 1957. A paddle-steamer can be seen approaching Birnbeck Pier.

A SWALLOW DIVE from the boards at the open-air swimming-pool, 1951. The swimming-pool was opened in 1937. The diving-board was built of reinforced concrete by George Pollard & Co. Ltd of Taunton. It was then renowned as Europe's finest diving-stage.

ANOTHER VIEW of the diving-boards and fountain, 1954. The boards became unsafe and were demolished in 1982, prior to the swimming-pool's transformation into the Tropicana.

WESTON SEA FRONT from the diving-board at the open-air swimming-pool, 1959. The white building to the right of the Grand Atlantic Hotel is a bandstand.

BEACH ROAD from the diving-board at the crowded open-air swimming-pool, 1959. The large white house is Etonhurst. After much debate and planning enquiries, it was demolished in the 1970s.

A CONTESTANT in the Modern Venus beauty competition at the open-air swimming-pool.

THE WINTER GARDENS, 1959. The pianist in the bandstand is Eric Lamb.

MISS JACKIE PETERSON of Chelmsford was the winner of the Modern Venus beauty competition in 1959.

THE WINTER GARDENS PAVILION from the General Post Office, 1954. The poster on the left of the building is advertising Elsie and Doris Waters at Knightstone Theatre.

THE WINTER GARDENS PAVILION at night. The lights were installed in 1950, as part of a new sea-front illumination scheme.

ANOTHER VIEW of the Winter Gardens Pavilion at night. These photographs show the building before the columns were filled in to provide space for a café.

THE FRONT of the Winter Gardens Pavilion, 1950.

THE LILY POND in the Winter Gardens, 1959.

THE HIGH STREET and Winter Gardens lily pond from the Pavilion, 1952. To the left can be seen the bombed site of Lance & Lance's store being used as a car park. Lance's are operating from temporary buildings next to Walker & Ling.

THE WINTER GARDENS TENNIS COURTS, 1954. The Grand Pier Pavilion can be seen to the left.

A KINDLY POLICEMAN takes charge of this lost child, 9 June 1957.

HOTEL VILLA ROSA, from the town guide, 1951. This Italianate mansion was built in 1844. In 1969, after several years of discussions about the type of development to take place, plans were approved for two blocks of flats and Villa Rosa was demolished.

THE CAIRO HOTEL, 1951. Now called the Chairman's Choice Hotel, the original building was erected in 1821 and was called Devonshire Cottage. It was bought by Thomas Roblyn, a retired naval surgeon, who renamed it Cairo Lodge, as he had been present at the taking of Cairo during the Battle of the Nile. It underwent many alterations and additions and became a hotel in the 1920s. From 1940 to 1942 it was occupied by the Brigade of Guards and, for the rest of the war, by the US Marine Corps. Well into the 1970s I remember it for its superb Art Deco front doors with scenes of camels and pyramids etched on to the glass.

THE GRAND CENTRAL HOTEL, 1955. The first part of this hotel was built in 1925. It was designed to be built in three phases, each time adding a storey. The third phase was, however, never built.

SECTION TWO

Transport

ENGINE MAINTENANCE in Weston's railway yards, 1956.

LOCKING ROAD MISSION HALL. This hall was built in the 1850s by the Bristol & Exeter Railway Co. It was to provide shelter and refreshment to excursion passengers and therefore free the main station, then situated in Alexandra Parade, for regular traffic.

THE GOODS STATION, Locking Road. The building on the extreme left was originally the stables for the Great Western Railway. The tiny building on the right was a governor house belonging to the gas company.

THE 8.00 A.M. PLYMOUTH TO LIVERPOOL TRAIN passes Weston-super-Mare signal-box on 12 October 1954.

LOCKING ROAD EXCURSION STATION. The fine, stone horse trough is a reminder of earlier forms of transport.

THE BEACH LAWNS from the Beach Hotel, 1953. Most of these coaches would have belonged to Bakers, whose office appears on the left of this photograph.

THE BEACH BUS STATION AND CAFÉ, 1950. The buses at this time were operated by the Bristol Tramways and Carriage Co. Ltd. Note the petrol pumps outside the entrance.

ANOTHER VIEW of the bus station which was demolished in January 1988. Carlton Mansions now occupies the site.

SILVER SAILS TAXIS. They were in the High Street, opposite West Street. The garage is now the Tudor Market.

A ROAD ACCIDENT, Sunday 20 July 1958. This collision on the corner of Clevedon and Walliscote Roads, involved two cars and a cyclist, Mrs Hicks. PC Davis is seen here taking a statement from one of the drivers.

OUTSIDE GERMAN'S GARAGE, Milton Road, 3 June 1958. Heavy rain, combined with a high tide of 39 ft 2 in caused flooding. This photograph was taken at 7.30 p.m., half an hour before high tide.

PS *GLEN GOWER* approaching Birnbeck Pier, August 1953. *Glen Gower* was the first steamer built for P & A Campbell after the First World War, and was launched in 1922. Her distinguished war service included evacuating 1,235 men from Dunkirk. She was withdrawn in 1957 and sold for scrap three years later.

CAPTAIN GEORGE on the bridge of the PS *Bristol Queen* as she approaches Birnbeck Pier landing-stage, 1958.

BIRNBECK PIER, C. 1958. Passengers disembark from one of P & A Campbell's paddle-steamers.

BIRNBECK PIER, 1957. A paddle-steamer is waiting at the jetty. In earlier times trams would have been lined up where the cars are parked to transport the boat's passengers into the town.

Town Life

WESTON-SUPER-MARE from the Grand Atlantic Hotel, 1958.

AN AERIAL VIEW of Marine Lake and the hillside. This photograph was taken on Sunday 15 June 1958. There is not a single block of flats in sight!

CLAREMONT CRESCENT, 1957. The lamp-posts originally carried tram cables.

MADEIRA ROAD, 1957, looking north with South Road in the distance.

THE PUTTING GREEN in the Winter Gardens, 1953. In this view taken from the General Post Office, you can see that bomb damage to buildings on the corner of Waterloo Street has left the side wall of the London Hotel exposed.

THE CORNER of Waterloo Street and the High Street. Lance & Lance's store was on the right, but received a direct hit during the war. On the left is the side wall of the London Hotel. New shops have already been built in Waterloo Street.

THE HIGH STREET from the Italian Gardens, 1952. On the left Lance & Lance are in temporary buildings.

ST JAMES STREET, looking south. The buildings on the left are the Bristol Co-operative Society's dairy, drapery and mantle shops.

OXFORD STREET from the sea front, 1955. Nearly every building on the right-hand side of the road has been demolished. Dolphin Square now occupies much of the site.

THE HIGH STREET from the roof of the Winter Gardens, 1952.

ALEXANDRA PARADE. Orchard Street is on the left past the half-timbered building.

ALEXANDRA PARADE. The Railway Hotel is on the right, and public toilets can be found behind the taxi drivers' shelter.

REGENT STREET, C. 1958.

THE FLORAL CLOCK, 1956. This design, by Parks Superintendent J. Swift, was to celebrate the clock's twenty-first anniversary. It was laid out by Arthur Dunston with nearly forty thousand plants, including begonias, geraniums and lobelia, and took three weeks to plant.

CORONATION ESTATE, 1959. The foundations of the houses have just been laid in the lower left of this photograph. These were gradually replacing the rows of 'prefabs', distinguishable by their light-coloured roofs.

KNIGHTSTONE ROAD. The large building in the centre is St John's School. This was built in 1847 as the National School, run by the Church of England. It has now been demolished and the site is occupied by the Technical College which opened in 1970.

REGENT STREET. The ornate building in the centre of this photograph is the Plough Hotel, demolished in 1972 for Marks & Spencer's extension (see also p. 154).

ORCHARD STREET, 1955. Vernon Goold's Estate Agency was at No. 33. Mr Goold was also a councillor and was the last mayor of Weston before local government reorganization in 1974.

STATION ROAD, 1958. The Magistrates' Court can be seen in the centre of this photograph with the Victoria Methodist Church on the left. This church was built in 1931 after the original one was destroyed by fire.

THE CENTRE, 1957. The Bristol & Exeter pub on the corner was so named because it was close to Weston's second railway station built in 1866 by the Bristol & Exeter Railway Co. where Tesco's store is now. The pub was renamed the Town Crier in 1978.

GROVE PARK AND GROVE HOUSE, 1952. This house was the summer home of the Smyth-Pigott family of Brockley, who were the lords of the manor of Weston. The house was severely damaged during the war by incendiary bombs on the night of 4 January 1941, and again in June 1942. Most of it was later demolished. Only the coach house remains today, with a new extension built on the east side, to serve as the Mayor's Parlour.

ALEXANDRA PARADE, 1957. Quite a few changes have taken place since this photograph was taken. The iron railings have gone, along with some of the houses on the right. The cast-iron lamp-posts once carried tram cables.

A WINTRY DAY in Ashcombe Park, 1950.

THE DRINKING FOUNTAIN in Grove Park, 1956.

THE BOULEVARD. Orchard Street is on the right next to the chapel (see also p. 75).

THE BOULEVARD. Most of the buildings on the north side of the road were intended as domestic dwellings. Some of them are shown here being converted into shops and offices.

ATLANTIC ROAD, 1957. The church in the centre is Holy Trinity. It was built in 1861 to serve the fashionable, hillside, residential area built around the same time. The church was made redundant in March 1983 and was reopened three years later as the Elim Pentecostal Church.

THE BOULEVARD CONGREGATIONAL CHURCH, c. 1958. This church was officially opened in 1959, exactly seventeen years after the destruction of the original building, which was hit by incendiary bombs on the the morning of Sunday 27 June 1942. The new church is of a modern open-plan design, but laid on the original foundations.

THE BOULEVARD METHODIST CHURCH. This was built in 1875 on the corner of Orchard Street. When the congregational church was bombed (see left below), the congregation shared this church, later renting it from the Methodists. In the basement was a hall and classroom which occasionally flooded at high tide. The church was used until 1959. It is now an estate agency.

COUNTY YOUTH HOBBIES EXHIBITION, Weston Museum, 1953. This show displayed the work of the first- and second-class award winners in a competition open to young people aged between fifteen and twenty-one.

WESTON LIBRARY, The Boulevard, c. 1957.

NEEDLEWORK in Somerset schools. Part of an exhibition at Weston Museum in February 1953, which displayed work by girls of eleven years and over from schools all over Somerset.

FLAGSELLER in the High Street. The flags were being sold in aid of Sunflower Day for Homeless and Destitute Children. The women were standing outside Carwardines, where various blends of tea have been displayed.

DROVE ROAD RAILWAY BRIDGE. The gas works are on the left.

BABY COMPETITION, 19 June 1958. Miss Zoe Newton judged these two the winners. The show was being held as part of National Milk Week.

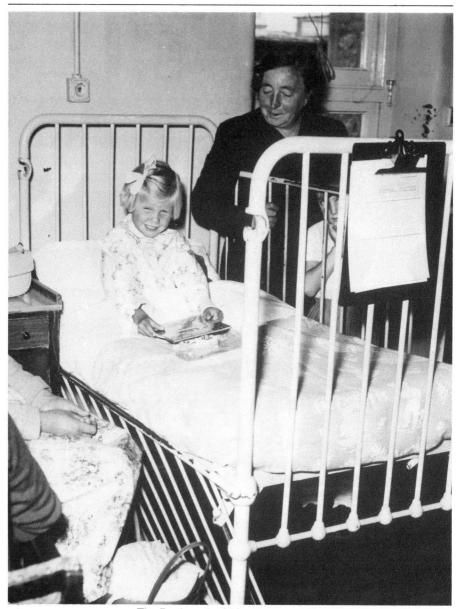

WESTON GENERAL HOSPITAL, The Boulevard, 1958, with a young patient in the childrens' ward.

SECTION FOUR

Coronation Celebrations

THE FLORAL CLOCK, 1953. This design included flags, the royal coat of arms and two portraits of the queen.

THE ROYAL ARCADE, decorated with bunting and flags. The shop on the left is selling seaside goodies such as postcards, rock, souvenirs, tin buckets and shrimp nets.

MEADOW STREET from Regent Street. These are very elaborate decorations, with printed banners, crowns and flags.

THE ODEON CINEMA, 1953. The film showing was *The Lusty Men*.

ST JAMES STREET, 1953. On the right is an unspoiled row of Edwardian shop fronts. At the end of the road, in Regent Street, is the Plough Hotel (see also p. 154).

THE HIGH STREET. Trevors' was demolished in 1990. The site will form an entrance to the Sovereign Centre, a new shopping complex.

ANOTHER VIEW of the High Street. The gap behind the hoardings in the centre is where Marks & Spencer's store was before it suffered bomb damage. It was rebuilt on the same site.

SANDFORD ROAD SPORTS, 1953. These were part of the street-party celebrations.

DANCING to the band in Grove Park to celebrate the coronation.

SECTION FIVE

Shopping

COUCH'S SHOP, St James Street, C. 1958. This shop was the main stockist of local school uniforms.

MEADOW STREET. These shops were on the south side of the road, near Regent Street. They were demolished for road improvements in 1967.

NORMAN & SON'S GROCERY SHOP. This stood opposite the High Street, on the eastern corner of Union Street (see also p. 151).

WIDGERY'S CHEMIST SHOP. This was on the corner of West Street and Lower Church Road. It is still a chemists. Although this photograph was taken in the early 1960s, the shop front remained unchanged from the early years of the century. The door, brass signs and many of the shop contents can now be seen in Woodspring Museum, Weston.

THE HIGH STREET, looking south in 1954. Notice the banner on the left, advertising the RAFA Battle of Britain Week.

THE HIGH STREET, C. 1958. There is a fine variety of old shop fronts here, especially the gilded wood and glass sign over Boots. W.H. Smith & Son were holding a book sale, with prices ranging from 2s. (10p) to 5s. (25p).

THE HIGH STREET. This photograph was taken at the same time as the one above, but showing shops a little further along the road.

THE HIGH STREET, 1957. In the distance is the newly-widened High Street South, once Union Street. The new Government offices are taking shape under scaffolding. These were due for occupancy by the Inland Revenue, National Assistance Board, Customs & Excise and Ministries of Labour, Transport and Pensions.

OXFORD STREET, looking east.

REGENT STREET, looking west. The entrance to the Grand Pier is at the end of the road.

REGENT STREET, looking east. All the buildings on the right-hand side of the road have since been demolished. The 'Road-Up' sign is at the old narrow entrance to Union Street.

THE LINGERIE COUNTER at Walker & Ling, High Street, c. 1950.

MARKS & SPENCER'S, 1958. A sale at the millinery counter has attracted a crowd.

THE STOCKING COUNTER at Marks & Spencer's on 31 July 1958.

REGENT STREET, looking west. The building in the distance on the right is Burton's menswear shop.

MEADOW STREET, looking east. The turning on the left is North Street.

THE MAGIC OF TELEVISION. This set, in the window of 19 Meadow Street, has attracted a large audience. Even the roadsweeper has stopped to watch. This photograph was taken on 7 March 1957.

OXFORD STREET, c. 1954. The building on the right is the Three Queens Hotel on the corner of Union Street, now High Street South.

REGENT STREET. P.C. Wall was a fishmonger. All these shops have now been demolished. Inshops now occupies the site.

ST JAMES STREET. Bart's Stores was on the corner of Richmond Street. Notice the delivery boy's bicycle leaning against the wall.

ORCHARD PLACE. This old-fashioned corn chandler's is selling everything from fruit, vegetables, seeds and flowerpots to live chickens and budgerigars.

LANCE & LANCE in the High Street. Notice the fine pineapples on the parapet of the building on the left. They were undoubtedly made at the Royal Pottery in Weston in the nineteenth century.

Weston at Play

WESTON AIRPORT, August 1958. Passengers are boarding for a pleasure flight. It cost 10s. (50p) for a circuit of Weston, 15s. (75p) to fly over Weston, Sandbay and Kewstoke, and £1 to fly over Cheddar Gorge, Clevedon or Burnham-on-Sea.

WESTON OPERATIC SOCIETY, April 1951. The cast are pictured here at Knightstone Theatre in a production of *Yeoman of the Guard*.

WILL HAMMER AND MICHEL KEBBY'S 'Sunshine Pierrots'. This group was performing at the Cove Pavilion in 1954.

THE WINTER GARDENS, 1959. Eric Lamb is the pianist in this bandstand in the Winter Gardens. Part of the old General Post Office can be seen in the background (see also p. 38).

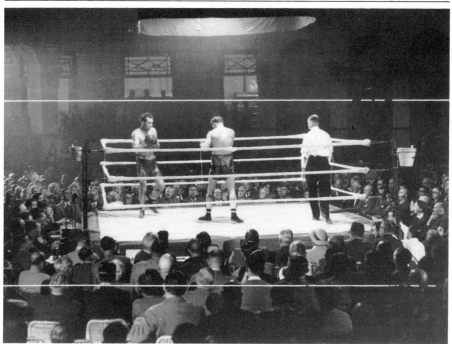

A TELEVISED BOXING TOURNAMENT at the Winter Gardens, 1953.

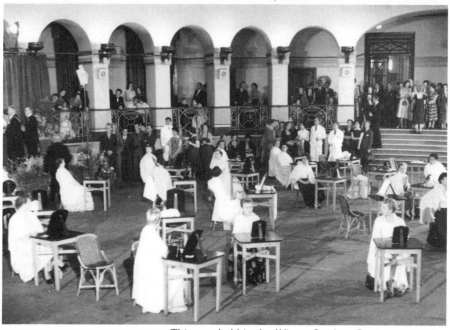

A TELEVISED HAIR-STYLING CONTEST. This was held in the Winter Gardens Pavilion in 1953.

THE 6-5 SPECIAL. This was the first music programme on television for teenagers. Broadcast from the Winter Gardens, this edition was introduced by Pete Murray and Jo Douglas. It featured Ken Mackintosh and his Orchestra and the Ray Ellington Quartet with Val Masters. It was filmed on 15 February 1958.

THE J. BAKER JAZZ GROUP. Teenagers dancing at Club 13 at the RAF Association Club in Grove Road, 1958.

THE FOUR STAR ballroom-dancing competition at the Winter Gardens, 1953.

A DANCE CLASS at Whitecross Hall, 1957. Mr Trevor Schofield is teaching these beginners ballroom dancing. During the 1950s about five million people went ballroom dancing each week.

TREVOR BROOKES and his Broadcasting Orchestra at the Winter Gardens Pavilion, 1953.

TRINITY BOYS CHOIR at the Winter Gardens, December 1952. They were being filmed for the television programme *Sunday Pops*.

CHRYSANTHEMUM SHOW, November 1952. This is the Corporation Parks Department exhibit.

THE CHRYSANTHEMUM SHOW, 1952. This show was held annually at the Winter Gardens. Here, Mr Rendell, Mr Goldstone and another judge discuss one of the entries.

ASHCOMBE PARK. A leisurely game of bowls whiles away this afternoon of June 1953.

THE ANNUAL BOWLS TOURNAMENT, 26 June 1958. Some players are pondering the result.

WESTON GOLF CLUB, June 1958. The cranes in the background were being used to lay the new town sewer.

THE WINTER GARDENS TENNIS COURTS, 1952. South Parade can be seen behind the trees.

THE SUMMER CARNIVAL, 19 June 1958. This 'Arabian Nights' float is passing down Regent Street.

THE BARBECUE on the Beach Lawns after the Summer Carnival, 19 June 1958. The Grand Atlantic Hotel is in the background.

SECTION SEVEN

Schools

THE WOODWORKING SHOP at the Grammar School for Boys, June 1958. From left to right are: R.J. Hancock, B.G. Taylor, Mr A. Robinson and R. Balfour.

A PUPIL OF CLASS 2B at Walliscote Road Junior School, 24 April 1958.

CLASS 1C at Walliscote Road Junior School, 24 April 1958.

A DOMESTIC SCIENCE LESSON at Weston Grammar School for Girls.

A CHEMISTRY LESSON at the Grammar School for Girls. The teacher is Brenda Norman.

WALLISCOTE ROAD JUNIOR SCHOOL, 4 July 1957. Children dance round the maypole at their school pageant.

WALLISCOTE ROAD. Mrs Evans, the lollipop lady, outside Walliscote Road Junior School at 3.30 p.m. on 14 September 1958.

Weston at Work

BRITANNIA AIRLINERS at Weston Airport, 1957. These 70-ton aircraft were the largest ever to land at the airfield. They came to Weston for modifications by Western Airways Ltd, prior to delivery to BOAC. As you can see there were problems fitting them into the hangars.

MR A. HAINES MAKING ROCK at W. Browning's factory in Stanley Road on 15 April 1958.

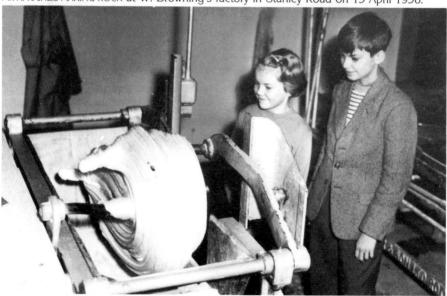

YOUNG VISITORS watch the rock being mixed.

ANOTHER STAGE in making seaside rock at Browning's.

THE FINISHED PRODUCT.

THE ROYAL POTTERIES. Left: the clay is being checked for consistancy. Right: a potter is demonstrating hand-throwing a flowerpot.

THE ROYAL POTTERIES, 1951. This is the modelling and mould-making shop.

THE NO. 6 POT-MAKING SHOP at the Royal Potteries, 1951. After being Weston's second main industry after tourism in the nineteenth century, the pottery began to lose staff to the new, cleaner light industries starting up in the town. Ten years after these pictures were taken the firm was forced into closure ending over 120 years of clayworking in Weston.

THE ROYAL POTTERIES, 1951. Perforated wire-cut bricks were a speciality at this time.

HENLY'S FACTORY, OLDMIXON. This was a Ministry of Supply works operated by Henley's from 1948 to 1965. Here, combat vehicles of all types, from RAF refuellers to DUKW amphibians, underwent a complete overhaul or rebuild.

HENLY'S FACTORY, OLDMIXON. The chassis assembly line.

H.E. BRYANT'S MOTOR BODY WORKS, Oxford Street, 17 August 1958. Arthur Shenton is working on a burnt-out ambulance under the supervision of H. Bryant (right).

C. & J. CLARK'S SHOE FACTORY. This is the sewing room at the Whitecross Road works, Thursday 10 July 1958.

WESTON GAS WORKS in Drove Road. Coal for gas production was delivered directly by rail. Production here ceased in 1968.

WESTLAND'S FACTORY, OLDMIXON. The No. 2 ground-testing rig, c 1957.

FRED MUDGE at work in the GPO sorting office, 14 April 1958.

MOORLAND LAUNDRY, Moorland Road, 1958. Starched shirt collars are being laid out for pressing. An old iron mangle is in the background on the right.

CORPORATION REFUSE COLLECTORS empty bins in St James Street, 15 April 1958.

MRS B. HUNTER at a switchboard in the telephone exchange, 14 April 1958. Up until 1969 all calls to and from Weston were handled by two manual exchanges. One was in the General Post Office and had 2,600 subscribers; the other was in The Boulevard and had 5,300 subscribers.

A GOOD DAY'S CATCH. Jack and Alf Payne unload barrels of sprats at Knightstone Harbour, 1958.

KNIGHTSTONE HARBOUR, 1958. Mr Carter is spreading his fishing nets out to dry.

A RAG-AND-BONE MAN'S CART in York Street.

DRAIN CLEANING in St James Street, 15 April 1958. The sweet shop in the background is advertising Fruit Rock at 6d. (2½p) and Fruit Baskets at 1s. (5p).

THE HIGH STREET, with resurfacing work underway. In the background work has started on rebuilding shops on the Lance & Lance site.

THE FLORAL CLOCK, May 1958. Gardeners from the Corporation Parks Department at work in Alexandra Parade.

Public Service

MAYOR MAKING AT THE TOWN HALL, 22 May 1958. From left to right: Cllr Mrs Grey, Cllr Lt. Col. Grey, Cllr L. Holtby (Mayor), Mrs Holtby.

THE TWENTY-FIRST ANNIVERSARY of the granting of the charter. Weston achieved Borough status in 1937. Here, the Apprentices' Band from RAF Locking march past the civic party outside the Winter Gardens, 1958.

THE TWENTY-FIRST ANNIVERSARY of the granting of the charter, 1958. The civic party enters the Winter Gardens Pavilion after a special church service.

THE TWENTY-FIRST ANNIVERSARY of the granting of the charter. Dignitaries arrive at the parish church for the special service, 1958. From left to right: Mrs Lickfold, Lady Alexander, Lord Alexander. The latter was born in George Street, Weston. He served as First Lord of the Admiralty during the Second World War.

THE PARADE to mark the anniversary of the Battle of Britain, 1958. Flight Officer MacDonald leads a flight from RAF Locking.

MEMBERS AND CHIEF OFFICIALS of Weston Borough Council, 1951. Back row, left to right: I. Davies, E. Turner, Cllr Geeve, H. Alletson, J. Freer-Hewish, Cllr Wadham, L. Jeffrey, Cllr Ivens, W. Bryant, A. Milton, B. Flavell, Cllr Staples. Middle row, left to right: A. Pritchard (mace bearer), Cllr Deane, Cllr Holtby, Cllr Tait, Cllr Lt. Col. Grey, Cllr Holcombe, Cllr Mrs Grey, Cllr Mrs Battiscombe, Cllr Rasey, Cllr Bessell, Cllr Miller-Barstow, Cllr Couch, Cllr Moor. Front row, left to right: Preb. Salmon, Ald Brown, Ald Heybyrne, Ald Barclay (deputy Mayor), Mrs Proctor (Mayoress) Ald Proctor (Mayor), R. Lickfold, Ald Bosley, Ald Dodgson, Cllr Mrs Lucas, Revd Carpenter.

ROYAL VISIT, 23 May 1953. Princess Margaret greets Lord Hylton, the Lord Lieutenant of Somerset, on her arrival in a Viking of the Queen's Flight. She was the first member of the Royal Family to land at Weston Airport.

ROYAL VISIT, 23 May 1953. Princess Margaret at the airport with the Lord Lieutenant of Somerset. She came to inspect Youth Services Units at RAF Locking Radio School and to see demonstrations by Somerset Youth Organizations at the Grammar School.

WESTON TOWN HALL, Walliscote Road, 1958.

WESTON LIFEBOAT, 1956. This launch was part of a combined exercise with other rescue units.

THE WAR MEMORIAL, Grove Park. This memorial to the local dead of the Second World War was unveiled and dedicated by Lord Hylton, the Lord Lieutenant of Somerset, on 8 March 1953.

THE TOWN CHRISTMAS TREE, 1951. This 50-ft fir came from the Luttrell Estate at Dunster, Somerset. The *Noah's Ark* from the Marine Lake (see p. 25) was placed alongside for the reception of gift parcels to supplement the Mayor's Christmas Fund.

SECTION TEN

Going, Going, Gone!

THIS MAP may help you to locate many of the backstreets pictured in the following chapter. (Reproduced from the Ordnance Survey map of 1911.)

CARLTON STREET, looking east, 1959.

COOPERS ARMS, Carlton Street. The owners are moving out prior to its demolition. Just over the top of the removal van you can see the Prince of Wales pub, which is still there. The narrow alley beside the Coopers Arms led to Maine Square.

CARLTON STREET, looking west. Some of these early nineteenth-century houses were quite elegant and were typical of seaside architecture of that period. The dark building facing the camera is Shaddick's Cottages.

ANOTHER VIEW OF CARLTON STREET, looking west towards the sea front.

WILCOX PLACE. These cottages were up an alley off Regent Street, just opposite the Railway Hotel (now Carriages of Weston).

SIDMOUTH COTTAGES, c. 1957.

NEW STREET, looking south. The Prince of Wales pub is at the end of the road in Carlton Street.

THE DEMOLITION of Nos 31, 35 and 37 Carlton Street, on the corner of Castle Street, is in progress on 25 September 1958.

CASTLE STREET, looking south. The infant school is at the end of the road.

ANOTHER VIEW OF CASTLE STREET, looking south.

CASTLE STREET, looking north.

THE CASTLE CAFÉ and Restaurant, Castle Street.

ANOTHER VIEW of the clearance area. Does anyone have any more information?

UNION STREET.

UNION STREET, looking north. The High Street is in the distance. This warehouse belonged to Thomas Govier, Fruit and Potato Merchant.

Left: LAURA BUILDINGS. These cottages were off Regent Street. Emmanuel Church Tower is in the background. Right: THE FIRE STATION in Oxford Street, next to the Central Cinema.

NORTH STREET. Part of this street was standing until 1978 when it was widened to provide better access to the rear of the High Street.

THE CENTRAL CINEMA, Oxford Street. At this time there were two other cinemas in the town – the Odeon in the centre and the Regent (later the Gaumont) in Regent Street. As television grew in popularity so cinema audiences declined. Between 1954 and 1959 more than eight hundred cinemas were forced to close.

OXFORD STREET looking east. None of the buildings on the right still stand.

THE QUEEN'S HOTEL, Regent Street. The floodlit building on the left is the Central Cinema.

THE QUEEN'S HOTEL. This was on the corner of Regent Street and Union Street. The site is now occupied by Superdrug.

REGENT STREET, 1957. Norman & Son's grocery shop is empty prior to demolition (see also p. 89). To the right is the newly-widened High Street South, once Union Street.

REGENT STREET, looking west. This is a different view of the buildings shown in the photograph above.

THE WEST SIDE of Castle Street during demolition, 25 September 1958. A Rover car is being loaded with salvaged timber.

THE REMAINS of Union Street, 8 June 1958.

BEACH ROAD. The Oxford Street turning is on the left. Most of these buildings have gone. The Sands Restaurant and a petrol station occupy much of this site.

BEACH ROAD. The Cambridge Hotel and Nos 19 and 20, photographed on 15 December 1952. These buildings can also be seen in the picture above.

LOCKING ROAD. C.E. Carpenter & Son's monumental mason's workshop. They moved to the corner of Burlington Street and Alfred Street when this building was demolished.

THE PLOUGH HOTEL in Regent Street. This was demolished in 1972 to make way for the extension to Marks & Spencer's.

Out and About

THE KEWSTOKE TOLL-GATE, 1957. The gas lighting was still in use.

SAND BAY, 1957. The Kewstoke Convalescent Home is in the distance. The old smugglers' cottages on the left were converted into the Commodore Hotel in the 1960s. One of the first holiday chalets can be seen in the centre.

KEWSTOKE, 1958. Note the gas street lamp.

THE MOBILE LIBRARY at Worle, C. 1958. This was the first mobile library to serve any town in the south-west. It was opened in April 1957. The articulated vehicle was 30 ft long, including the cab, and cost £4,000. Three thousand new books were bought for it, with a further two thousand kept in reserve.

LAUREL FARM CARAVAN PARK, Worle.

ST NICHOLAS CHURCH, Uphill, 1957.

UPHILL VILLAGE from the hill, 1953.

OLD CHURCH ROAD, Uphill, 1954. The remains of the old windmill can be seen on the hill.

OLD CHURCH ROAD, Uphill, 1954. Ellesmere Road leads off on the left, with Uphill Tea Gardens in the centre. Note the gas street lighting.

ACKNOWLEDGEMENTS

I would like to express my thanks to the Curator of Woodspring Museum, Weston-super-Mare, for again allowing me to use photographs from their collection, including some of the pictures donated to the museum by Mr Sandys.

I am also indebted to Mr M. Tozer, Mr E.C. Amesbury, and the unknown photographers whose work I have included.

Finally my thanks to my mother for her help and encouragement.

I hope I have avoided any inaccuracies in the captions. As always, I would be happy to receive any further infomation you may have about the photographs.